DEC 17 '14

Khoury, Marielle D.,
   1969-

Henry Purcell.

$19.99

D1032846

DATE			

ISBN 1 85103 309 2

Originally published as *Henry Purcell Découverte des Musiciens* jointly by Editions Gallimard Jeunesse & Erato Disques.

© & ℗ 1999 by Editions Gallimard Jeunesse & Erato Disques.

This edition first published in the United Kingdom jointly by Moonlight Publishing Ltd. The King's Manor. East Hendred. Oxon OX12 8JY
& The Associated Board of the Royal Schools of Music (Publishing) Limited. 24 Portland Place. London W1B 1LU.

English text © & ℗ 2001 by Moonlight Publishing Ltd & The Associated Board of the Royal Schools of Music.

Printed in Italy by Editoriale Libraria.

Henry

PURCELL

FIRST DISCOVERY - MUSIC

Written by Marielle D. Khoury
Illustrated by Charlotte Voake
Narrated by Michael Cantwell

In the seventeenth century London was already a big, noisy city, bustling with life. The River Thames, running through the middle of it, was dotted with great sailing ships and teeming with little boats, shuttling back and

CITY SOUNDS

Do you live in a city or in the country? Have you noticed how different the sounds are when you are in a big city or in a little town, a village or out in the country?

1 THE FAIRY QUEEN, FIRST MUSIC: PRELUDE
DIDO AND AENEAS, SAILOR'S SONG 'COME AWAY'

forth. Henry Purcell was born in 1659, close to Westminster Abbey on the north bank of the Thames. His family may have lived in one of the little houses which clustered around the imposing church.

Henry had the same first name as his father, who was the choirmaster at the Abbey. Both Henry's father and his Uncle Thomas were court musicians.

They played and sang at the splendid parties held at the palace of King Charles II. Through them Henry discovered the delights of music very early in life.

Today the Queen has a less important role to play than Charles II did in the time of Purcell. But life at the royal court is still very grand, with great ceremonies, impressive receptions and splendid balls. Listen to this court dance and see if you can find steps to suit the music.

9

Henry

enry was scarcely five when his father died. His mother was left with six children. Henry went to live with his Uncle Thomas, who from then on looked after his education. The following year the Great Plague struck

3 FUNERAL MUSIC FOR QUEEN MARY,
MARCH AND FUNERAL SENTENCE 'IN THE MIDST OF LIFE'

London. Within a few months thousands of people died of this terrible illness, which was incurable. A year later a great fire broke out, destroying a huge area of London yet killing only nine people.

MUSIC FOR ONLY ONE DAY

In Purcell's day recordings did not exist. Often a work of music would be played only once, perhaps for a birthday, a marriage or a funeral. Just imagine if you could only hear a song you like once! Would you remember it?

Henry was lucky enough to be admitted to the School of the Chapel Royal, a choir of men and boys. He was taught to sing, read music and to play the lute, the violin and the harpsichord. He also learnt to read and write like

12

4 ANTHEM
'MY HEART IS INDITING'

other children of his age. In their fine red choir robes Henry and his friends sang in church for King Charles and the royal court.

A SCHOOL WITH A DIFFERENCE

Today there are still special schools in England where children are taught to sing in choirs and these are known all over the world. Listen to this choral piece and try to follow the boys' treble parts, which are much higher than the lower men's voices.

Henry was thirteen when his voice broke and he had to leave the choir. He continued his musical training with his godfather, John Hingeston, the court organist.

5 TIMON OF ATHENS,
DUET 'HARK! HOW THE SONGSTERS'

Henry became his assistant and helped him maintain, repair and tune the royal keyboard and wind instruments. He also began to write music.

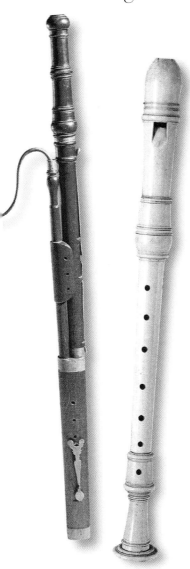

WIND INSTRUMENTS

The song you are about to hear is accompanied by two wind instruments: the recorder, which is high pitched, and the bassoon, which is much deeper. Which do you think sounds like birdsong?

By the following year Henry had proved his worth. He was taken on as the organ tuner at Westminster Abbey and began to earn his living. Through his work he became friends with the abbey organist and composer

A Song in the *Rival-Sisters.*

E—*lia* has a thouſand, thouſand, thou—

6 KING ARTHUR,
VENUS'S SONG 'FAIREST ISLE'

John Blow, who taught him to play the organ. Henry was only sixteen years old when one of his first compositions was published in a book of songs.

LYRICS AND TUNES

Do you know any songs in another language? You can quite easily make up your own words for a song if you like the tune but don't understand the words.

Henry was interested in all kinds of music. He developed a fascination for the theatre thanks to an old family friend, Matthew Locke, who wrote music for the

7 KING ARTHUR, TENOR ARIA 'COME IF YOU DARE'

first English operas. Some years later Henry would in his turn write some very fine operas, including *Dido and Aeneas* and *King Arthur*.

SHOUT FOR JOY

Listen to the Knights of the Round Table as they come on stage. You can hear them shouting and singing their victory song after battle. When you win a game, do you feel like shouting and singing for joy?

At eighteen, Henry was already well known and much appreciated at the court. He was appointed as court composer. Up until his death in 1695, he wrote music regularly for religious services, royal occasions, and also for theatre and opera in London. His music was to make him very famous throughout the country.

WHAT IS IN THE ORCHESTRA?

The court orchestra was known as the King's Violins. It combined several string instruments from the highest pitch to the lowest: violins, violas, cellos and double bass. See if you can recognize each one in this piece of music.

20

8 ODE 'COME, YE SONS OF ART, AWAY', OVERTURE

Today

as in the past

Purcell's

music

is played

and loved.

'MY BELOVED SPAKE'

Purcell composed many pieces for services in Westminster Abbey. Some were in Latin but most were works written in English for choir, and often solo voices. They are known as anthems and are usually accompanied by organ and sometimes by an orchestra. Some anthems are hymns to the glory of God, in which the voices rise joyously in celebration of the beauty of God's world and all his creatures. Other anthems are more serious and sombre. They express man's pain in the troubles of life or his sorrow at the loss of someone dear. These are prayers asking God for his support.

The organ as an instrument of the church plays a key part in religious music, either solo or as an accompaniment to choral music.

The Westminster Abbey choristers still wear robes just like those worn in Purcell's day.

22

9 ANTHEM 'MY BELOVED SPAKE'
ANTHEM 'HEAR MY PRAYER, O LORD'

ODE TO SAINT CECILIA

The life of the royal court was full of solemn occasions. Every year Purcell had to write an important composition, called an ode, for soloists, choir and orchestra to the glory of His Majesty the King. These odes celebrated certain events: the king's birthday, or his return to London after spending the summer in his country palace, or else the wedding of a member of the royal family. The finest odes are the ones Purcell wrote to celebrate the birthday of Queen Mary, who loved music and often invited Purcell to play for her. Purcell also composed odes in honour of Saint Cecilia, the patron saint of music. In these he celebrated the magic of voices and instruments.

Writing an ode was not simple because parts had to be created for many musicians and it had to be to the liking of the king and queen.

Queen Mary, whose husband was often absent, had to face political troubles on her own. She appreciated music all the more because it took her mind off such problems.

24

10 ODE 'COME, YE SONS OF ART, AWAY', DUET 'SOUND THE TRUMPET'
ODE 'HAIL, BRIGHT CECILIA', SOPRANO ARIA 'THOU TUN'ST THIS WORLD'

THE FAIRY QUEEN

Purcell worked a lot for London theatres. He was commissioned to write overtures and interludes to open and close the acts in tragedies or comedies, and sometimes to compose songs and dances for particular scenes. But Purcell's genius was revealed above all in his operas. *Dido and Aeneas* is a short, tragic work that tells of the love of Dido, Queen of Carthage, for the Trojan, Aeneas. Purcell's other operas are longer. Musical scenes alternate with spoken scenes. *The Fairy Queen* takes place in a magic forest. Each of the five acts finishes with a great, colourful, musical celebration, full of contrasting emotions that demonstrate the true richness of Purcell's music.

King Arthur was inspired by the Arthurian legend of the Knights of the Round Table. Aided by his magician, Merlin, Arthur must complete various tasks in order to find his fiancée, Emmeline, prisoner of the sorcerer, Osmond.

Actors, dancers, singers and musicians all took part in the shows, which were set to music by Purcell. The scenery was often sumptuous.

26

MOONLIGHT PUBLISHING

Translator:
Penelope Stanley-Baker

ABRSM (PUBLISHING) LTD

Project manager:
Leslie East

Assisted by:
Susie Gosling

Text editor:
Lilija Zobens

Editorial supervision:
Caroline Perkins & Rosie Welch

Production:
Simon Mathews

English narration recording:
Ken Blair of BMP Recording

ERATO DISQUES

Artistic and Production Director:
Ysabelle Van Wersch-Cot

LIST OF ILLUSTRATIONS

PHOTOGRAPHIC ACKNOWLEDGEMENTS

Archiv für Kunst und Geschichte, Paris **16t**, **19**, **25**, **26b**, **27**. Artephot/Bal **11**. Artephot/Bridgeman **6**, **24b**. Christie's Image Ltd 1999 **20**. Ph. Coqueux/Specto **24m**, **26t**, **26m**. Dean and Chapter of Westminster **12**, **22m**. D. R. **15l**, **15m**, **16b**, **22b**. A. F. Kersting **23**. By Courtesy of The National Portrait Gallery, London **9**, **21**. Pepys Library, Magdalene College, Cambridge **15r**. Photo R. M. N. – Jean Schormans **24t**. Pierre-Marie Valat **22t**.

CD

I. A city child
The Fairy Queen,
First Music: Prelude
The Amsterdam Baroque Orchestra
Directed by Ton Koopman
4509 98507 2
℗ Erato Disques S.A.. 1995
Coproduction Erato/Bull

Bull ◯

Dido and Aeneas,
Sailor's Song 'Come away'
Jean-Paul Fouchécourt. tenor
Les Arts Florissants
Directed by William Christie
4509 98477 2
℗ Erato Disques S.A.. 1995
Coproduction Erato/Pechiney

PECHINEY ≫

2. Like father, like son
Dido and Aeneas,
The Triumphing Dance
Les Arts Florissants
Directed by William Christie
4509 98477 2
℗ Erato Disques S.A.. 1995
Coproduction Erato/Pechiney

PECHINEY ≫

3. Dark days
Funeral Music for Queen Mary,
March and Funeral Sentence 'In the
midst of life'
Equale Brass Ensemble
Monteverdi Choir & Orchestra
Directed by John Eliot Gardiner
4509 96553 2
℗ Erato Classics SNC. 1977

4. Learn to read as you sing
Anthem 'My Heart is Inditing'
Choir of King's College. Cambridge
Leonhardt-Consort
Directed by Gustav Leonhardt
0630 17954 2
℗ Teldec Classics International. GmbH.
Hamburg. Germany 1970

5. In the service of the royal court
Timon of Athens,
Duet 'Hark! How the Songsters'
English Baroque Soloists

Directed by John Eliot Gardiner
4509 96556
℗ Erato Disques S.A.. 1988
Coproduction Erato/WDR

WDR

6. First job
King Arthur,
Venus's Song 'Fairest isle'
Véronique Gens. soprano
Les Arts Florissants
Directed by William Christie
4509 98535 2
℗ Erato Disques S.A.. 1995
Coproduction Erato/Pechiney/Châtelet

PECHINEY ≫   CHATELET

7. From church to theatre
King Arthur,
Tenor aria 'Come if you dare'
Iain Paton. tenor
Les Arts Florissants
Directed by William Christie
4509 98535 2
℗ Erato Disques S.A.. 1995
Coproduction Erato/Pechiney/Châtelet

PECHINEY ≫   CHATELET

8. Royal composer
Ode 'Come, ye sons of art, away',
Overture
Equale Brass Ensemble
Monteverdi Orchestra
Directed by John Eliot Gardiner
4509 96553
℗ Erato Disques S.A.. 1977

9. Sacred music
Anthem 'My beloved spake'
Charles Brett. countertenor
Wynford Evans. tenor
Stephen Varcoe. baritone
Roderick Earle. bass
Monteverdi Choir. English Baroque Soloists
Directed by John Eliot Gardiner
2292 45987 2
℗ Erato Disques S.A.. 1980

Anthem 'Hear my prayer, O Lord'
The Choir of New College, Oxford
Directed by Edward Higginbottom
3984 21659 2
℗ Erato Disques S.A.. 1998

10. The odes
Ode 'Come, ye sons of art, away',
Duet 'Sound the trumpet'
Charles Brett. John Williams,
countertenors
Monteverdi Orchestra
Directed by John Eliot Gardiner
4509 96553 2
℗ Erato Disques S.A.. 1977

Ode 'Hail, bright Cecilia',
Soprano aria 'Thou tun'st this
world'
Jennifer Smith. soprano
English Baroque Soloists
Directed by John Eliot Gardiner
4509 96554 2
℗ Erato Disques S.A.. 1983

II. Music for the theatre
Timon of Athens,
Curtain Tune
English Baroque Soloists
Directed by John Eliot Gardiner
4509 96556 2
℗ Erato Disques S.A.. 1988
Coproduction Erato/WDR

WDR

King Arthur,
Bass aria 'What power
art thou'
Petteri Salomaa. bass
Les Arts Florissants
Directed by William Christie
4509 98535 2
℗ Erato Disques S.A.. 1995
Coproduction
Erato/Pechiney/Châtelet

PECHINEY ≫   CHATELET

The Fairy Queen,
Final chorus 'They shall be as
happy'
Els Bongers. Catherine Bott.
sopranos; Michael Schopper. bass
The Amsterdam Baroque Orchestra
& Choir
Directed by Ton Koopman
4509 98507 2
℗ Erato Disques S.A.. 1995
Coproduction Erato/Bull

Bull ◯

JOHANN SEBASTIAN BACH
LUDWIG VAN BEETHOVEN
HECTOR BERLIOZ
FRYDERYK CHOPIN
CLAUDE DEBUSSY
GEORGE FRIDERIC HANDEL
WOLFGANG AMADEUS MOZART
HENRY PURCELL
FRANZ SCHUBERT
ANTONIO VIVALDI